The Frog Pond Dash

By Sascha Goddard

"Today we will run in the Frog Pond Dash," said Mog. "Just one frog can win."

The little frogs could not sit still.

"Good luck, frogs!" said Mog. "One, two, GO!"

The frogs jumped into the bog.

Thick mud stuck to them.

Then, it was the big jump.

“I can do it!” said Yog,
and she jumped the big gap.

Zog, Mog and Pog
jumped, too.

Then, the fog got thick.

Zog and Pog could not see the track ...

and they did not spot the big hog!

Zog and Pog ran from the hog.

They had to jog back into the bog!

Yog and Mog jumped up
on the log, then in the pond.

Yog could swim fast!

Yog wins the
Frog Pond Dash!

CHECKING FOR MEANING

1. What happened when the frogs first jumped into the bog? *(Literal)*
2. Who wins the Frog Pond Dash? *(Literal)*
3. Why do you think Zog and Pog ran from the hog? *(Inferential)*

EXTENDING VOCABULARY

Dash	Look at the word *Dash*. What does the word *Dash* mean? How many sounds can you hear in the word?
jumped	Look at the word *jumped*. What is the base of this word? How has adding *–ed* to the base changed the meaning? What other words can you think of where *–ed* is added to show that an action happened in the past?
hog	Look at the word *hog*. What does it mean? What is another word that has a similar meaning to *hog*?

MOVING BEYOND THE TEXT

1. Have you ever competed in a race or competition? How did you go?
2. How would you describe the hog in the story?
3. What other animals can jump?
4. Who do you think would enjoy this book? Why?

SPEED SOUNDS

PRACTICE WORDS

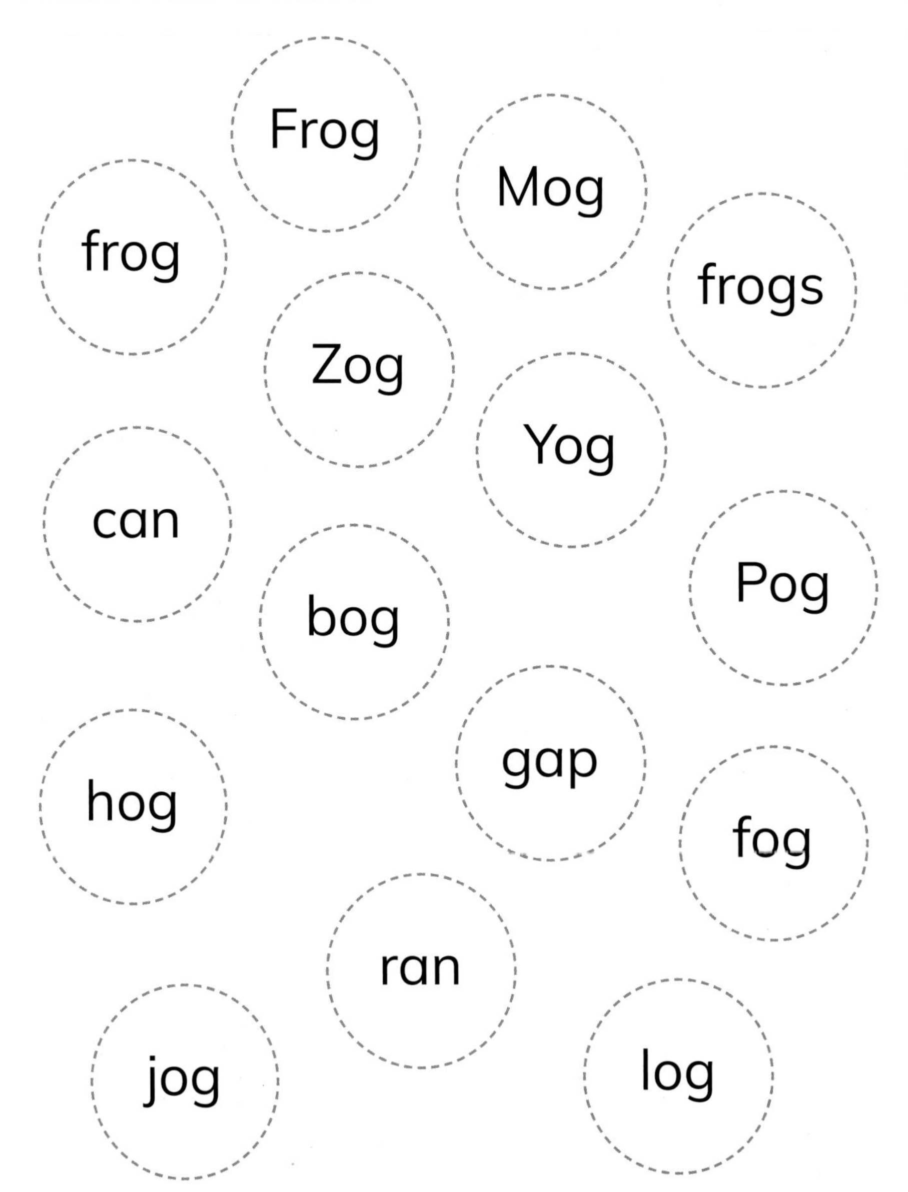